PSALMS
FROM MY SEVENTIES
AND OTHER STUFF

Janet invites us into her frank and wide-ranging conversations with God. If the church is a ship, these conversations are written from the life raft, by someone who was once a captain. From the grief of ageing and the fragility of happiness, to the delight of wine and blue tongue lizard's feet, and the reminder that we don't have to wait until New Year's to make new beginnings. Janet's psalms are vulnerable and empathetic, inviting tears and smiles amidst the uncertainty of an honest, open-hearted faith.

Rev Dr Jason John
Author, Poet, Finalist *Australian Poetry Slam 2019*
Forest Chaplain and Bellingen Landcare Coordinator]

Janet Dawson lives as she writes. In this book, she exemplifies a deep spirituality in the ordinariness of life, with prayers about the closed blinds ... sharing communion with a lizard ... shedding tears in the fragility of life ... reflecting on how hard it is to let go, especially to let go a life partner who is changing before her eyes. There is no pretence, no puffed-up terminology, no pious hope in these prayers; they are every day, grounded in the ordinary—and thus, so profound.

Janet especially grapples with her uncomfortableness—her sense of alienation—in the regular weekly routines of worship. Can there be a theology that offers something better than unthinking platitudes and unacceptable dogmas? Janet seeks to offer precisely this in her prayers, celebrating the music that has been "a joy and treasure all my life", remembering "those who can't rejoice", questioning "what did Jesus think he was doing?", imagining people as "beautiful round objects with so many exciting possibilities", offering images of God as "Quantum God, Eternal Becoming, Infinite Possibility, Ultimate Consciousness", and rejoicing as she leaves behind "the boat" of the church and immerses herself in "the Ocean" of the divine. And to close, a short, punchy drama about God in the ordinariness of life. Thank you, Janet.

Rev. Dr John Squires
Editor, *With Love to the World*
former Principal, Perth Theological Hall
former Presbytery Minister and Senior Lecturer in Biblical Studies

This broad-ranging collection of everyday psalms draws the reader/pray-er into many life situations that may initially seem trivial, but can cause confusion, anger or despair in those that experience them. The grief associated with ageing and dementia, the ephemeral nature of human happiness and the fragility and vulnerability of our natural world as we callously damage it along with the destructive force of racism are all identified and lifted up in prayer by Janet to the God of understanding presence. I loved Janet's honesty and vulnerability as she prays her faith and life.

Rev. Elizabeth Raine, retired Uniting Church Minister
Former Minister to Tuggeranong Uniting Church
Former Presbytery Minister, Mid North Coast Presbytery, NSW

PSALMS
FROM MY SEVENTIES
AND OTHER STUFF

JANET DAWSON

Published in Australia by
Coventry Press
33 Scoresby Road
Bayswater VIC 3153

ISBN 9781922589569

Copyright © Janet Dawson 2024

All rights reserved. Other than for the purposes and subject to the conditions prescribed under the *Copyright Act*, no part of this publication may be reproduced, stored in a retrieval system, or transmitted in any form or by any means, electronic, mechanical, photocopying, recording or otherwise, without the prior permission of the publisher.

Catalogue-in-Publication entry is available from the National Library of Australia
http://catalogue.nla.gov.au

Cover design by Ian James – www.jgd.com.au
Text design by Coventry Press
Set in EB Garamond

Printed in Australia

Contents

Foreword 7
   Ageing 9
   Australia Day 11
   Battle of the blinds 12
   Christmas 14
   Church's affirmation 16
   Confession 17
   Creature cousins 18
   Environment 20
   Evangelism 21
   Fear 23
   For the exiles 24
   Good Friday 25
   In the chapel 27
   Lent 5 28
   Letting go 29
   London Tower Block disaster (or Ukraine, or
   Palestine/Israel, or ...) 30
   Lonely 31
   Lord of the spheres 32
   Lunch 33
   May I know you 34
   Mental Health Week 35
   Mother's Day 36
   Music 37
   NAIDOC week 38
   New Year 40
   New Zealand, following the Christchurch mosque massacre .. 41
   No and yes 42
   Ocean 43
   Quantum God 46
   Remember! 48

Unbelief	49
World crises	50
Bring me a bottle	51
Cheap grace?	52
Decisions in Heaven, a play for Christmas	53
What is prayer?	59

Foreword

I've always been a writer; words seem to flow with greater fluency through my fingers than from my tongue. That's not to say I'm a tongue-tied, shrinking violet; I am also an actor and singer who loves an audience. A compulsive communicator, you might say. But to play with words, I need a pen in my hand or a keyboard beneath my fingers. Perhaps that is why God called me to ordained ministry, where these three skills have been incredibly useful. It was certainly counter-culture to the rest of my family.

During my training at United Theological College in Sydney, I was most fortunate to have Rev. Dr Graham Hughes as teacher of liturgical studies. Graham not only opened my eye to the depth and beauty of the traditions we have received, but encouraged me to use my own creativity in preaching and prayer. Graham, thank you.

At UTC, I was also introduced to journaling as an intentional spiritual practice. I already had notebooks full of journaling about my travels and life in general, so it was with enthusiasm and ease that I dived into this new pool.

Context is important, so I suppose I should tell you a little about myself. I am a retired Minister of the Word in the Uniting Church in Australia. I have also been a New Zealand School Dental Nurse, a waitress, a house cleaner, a secretary, and – in America – worked illegally packing meat in a supermarket.

The four countries I have lived in – as opposed to visited – are England, New Zealand, America and Australia. My husband, George, is a Texan, and we have two daughters and five grandchildren. We have been married 53 years at the time of writing. George is a lovely man and everything I have ever wanted in life I have because of him. He now has Alzheimer's, and this will be reflected in some of the writing. We currently live in Port Macquarie, New South Wales.

I am sharing these sometimes deeply personal reflections in the hope that they will be useful to others. Sometimes, putting things into words can help us clarify what is going on; that is why counselling or conversation with someone else works so well. But not everyone finds it easy to hit on the right words and perhaps these words will help. It is OK to be honest about what we really think and feel. Especially, to be honest with ourselves, and with God.

THANK YOU

To my mother, who could write a good story, song or poem and who must have passed on that gene to me. Thanks, Mum.

To all the faculty at Uniting Theological College 1986-1990. Before entering UTC, I would frequently have a dream where I was searching for a house. All the houses I entered were very small on the outside but extremely large on the inside; room after room unfolded before me as I walked. Those who analyse dreams sometimes say that a house represents yourself. After UTC, I never had that dream again.

To my colleagues and the members of the congregations I have served; thank you for helping me to learn my craft.

To my friends at Night4Murder Port Macquarie; thank you for performing my plays and making it so much fun!

To Kathy Luck, writer, artist and friend, for sharing her beautiful photographs.

To Hugh McGinlay at Coventry Press, who was gentle with my first timid offering and has led me through the publishing process with skill and kindness. You are the answer to prayer.

To all my family, especially my husband George and our daughters Diane and Christina, you have made my life worth living.

AGEING

Ageless God,
I don't like getting old,
I just don't relate to it at all.
In my mind, I'm still the youngest in the class.

It seems like only yesterday
I had to show ID to prove I was old enough,
now no-one even questions when I ask for Seniors' discount,
and shop assistants call me "Dear!"

I know I should be thankful, and I am.
I'm older (just) than my mother when she died.
My hair is still mostly brown, and I don't have arthritis.
But I'm getting long in the tooth – literally;
my dentist warns that my front teeth might fall out
if I don't change the way I brush.
And not only do I wear glasses, but now I'm getting cataracts.
Cataracts!
They happen to old people, and I just don't feel old.

But it's not just the physical ageing,
it's the aching sense of loss for all that is past
and can never be had again.
Never!

Never again will my parents welcome me with open arms.
Never again will my husband and I be young and carefree.
Never again will we walk hand in hand along the beach
feeling like Adam and Eve, ready to populate the world.
Never again will I feel a child stir within my womb,
feed a baby at my breast,
hear my children's laughter as they play in the sun.
Never.

At least, I can still remember,
some of us lose even memories.
Do you know what that is like, Ageless God?

When Jesus cried out in God-forsaken loneliness upon the cross,
was it this loss he felt?
Was he bearing, not our sins, but our terrible mortality?

So, do you know what it feels like to grow old, Ageless God?
You who exist from one eternity to the next, do you know?
Are you the Participating Presence as one by one
the things we treasure slip away?
Are they somehow held safe in you?

I hope so.

AUSTRALIA DAY

God of all the nations, today I need to pray for Australia
but I'm not quite sure how.
There are so many good things about Australia
and for these I am truly thankful.
And yet ...

Australia is the fourth country I've lived in;
we came here in 1983,
although it was 1996 before I became a citizen.
I think it's my home now.

How do I pray for a nation which let me in so quickly and easily
yet denies its blessings to those so much more needy than me
because they do not share my pale skin and English first language?

How do I pray for a nation whose First Peoples still struggle
for respect and recognition?

I have learned to love this ancient land.
The visit to Uluru and Kata Tjuta was inspirational
and impressed me with the land's fragility;
surely this is a land where we need to tread gently.
So, how do I pray for a nation where price and profit
are more important than environmental care?

This is the Lucky Country, so they say,
the land of the Fair Go.
But some of us have it a great deal fairer than others
and I'm one of them.
Each day, the news tells us how much our stocks are worth
and the state of our currency on the world market.
How do I pray for a nation where these are more important,
more newsworthy,
than how many are hungry, homeless, hopeless?

I can find only one prayer:
God, have mercy upon us.
Open our eyes, our minds, our hearts
to what we are doing.
Give us the wisdom, the courage, the humility
to be our best selves, not our worst.
May it be so.

BATTLE OF THE BLINDS

Bless me, Father, for I have sinned.
There has been another skirmish in the battle of the blinds.

You know how I love our light-filled home
with its big, wide windows.
I love to see the plants and trees,
the birds,
the sun and clouds and even the rain.

You know how I love to watch the sunset,
the glowing, changing colours,
the slow night fall,
the silhouette of trees against the dark sky,
the moon, the stars.

To shut out all this beauty with bland, white blinds,
I cannot do it.
But dear George can. And does.
Late afternoon or early evening,
come what may, despite my oft repeated pleas,
he closes up.

So ...
The other day I was in our bedroom,
(meditating!)
when I hear the swish of closing blinds.
This time I had no awareness of that moment of choice
between react and respond.
This time I leapt off the bed,
hurtled into the living room
and proceeded to lose my temper with satisfying thoroughness.

Satisfying only for the moment, of course.
After the blinds had been yanked open,
and in response to my shouted "Why?"
George had muttered something about the room not being complete,
I returned to the bedroom.

I felt such a failure,
as a wife, and as a meditator.

Why cannot I accept that he does not remember what I ask?
Why cannot I accept that this is what he will do?
When will this battle end?
God, show me what to do.

Oh!

Surrender.
This is the word You place inside my head.

I don't want to, You know that.
I really, really don't want to, but ...
That is the only way to end this battle.
Surrender.

OK.
So help me, God, to look at bland, white blinds
and be at peace.

CHRISTMAS

Hello, God.
I'm glad Christmas is over.
I just can't cope with all the hoo-hah any more.
I find it absolutely exhausting.
Each year, I fantasise about George and I going away somewhere by ourselves
but we never do.
Don't want to disappoint the kids and grandkids.
Ah well.

I didn't go to church – you know why.
That doesn't mean I didn't think about the gospel stories:
I did.
Late on Christmas Eve when the storm was raging
and the electricity was out
I stood at the window and watched the eastern sky ablaze with lightning.

I found myself singing the ancient words,
"And suddenly an angel of the Lord came upon them
and the glory of the Lord shone round about them, and they were sore afraid".

I found myself thinking about your messengers.
Some of them may light up the sky,
others may be more circumspect.

"For unto you is born this day in the city of David,
a Saviour, who is Christ the Lord."

I found myself thinking of my own baby born that very night
some 40 plus years ago.
Christina Marie; what else could we call her?

What a gift a child is, what a promise,
such a miraculous mingling of the dust of the earth and your divine spirit;
each and every one of them.
Very, very few children will light up the sky
yet they are all your children, and ours.

May we take better care of them,
may we teach them to love, not hate.
Then perhaps the song will be fulfilled,
"Peace on earth, good will to all".

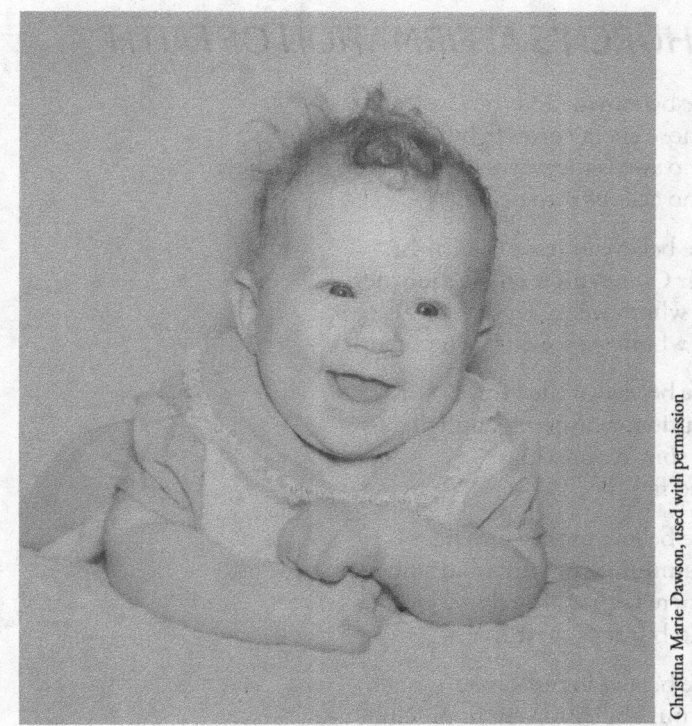

Christina Marie Dawson, used with permission

CHURCH'S AFFIRMATION OF FAITH

We believe in God the Creator,
whose energy gives light to the sun,
who swells the waves in their endless journey;
who calls us into being.

We believe in Jesus the Christ,
our Companion on life's journey;
in whom we see God,
in whom we see our own potential.

We believe in the Holy Spirit,
waiting, whispering, nudging us
to spread our wings
and fly!

We believe in the church,
community of saints and sinners;
where faith is grown
and burdens shared.

We believe in ourselves,
in our ability to wait upon God
and be transformed
into more than we ever dreamed possible.

Taken by Kathy Luck, used with permission

CONFESSION

Hello, God.
I'm having problems with the Prayers of Confession,
those endless and predictable lists
of the things we have or have not done.

I feel like getting up and shouting,
"Of course, we haven't done them!
We are fragile, needy creatures
and inside our head the primitive brain
with its relentless focus on sex and survival
is alive and well.
When are we going to talk about that?"

But, of course, I don't,
I'm too well trained in politeness.
I just get depressed,
fiddle with the news sheet,
look at my watch,
and wonder when the service will be over.

And when it finally is over
I go to my favourite coffee shop
gaze at the river
and put myself back together.

And this, God,
is my Prayer of Confession.

CREATURE COUSINS

Hello, God.
The most amazing thing happened at lunch today.
I was sitting out on my front porch,
munching my sandwich,
when I looked down to see a big blue-tongue lizard
just casually strolling past my chair.

We looked at each other, politely,
then, very slowly,
I put down a square of my cut-up papaya.

She,
(I don't know how to ascertain lizard gender,
but "it" seems rude),
anyway,
she cautiously flicked out her tongue,
contemplated my offering,
decided it was acceptable,
and daintily ate it.
(Definitely "she".)

I made another offering, tomato this time,
which was also accepted.

I went back to munching my sandwich.

Then, and this is the exciting part,
I felt a touch on my bare right foot.
She was checking out my toenails for edibility,
in the process climbing onto my foot.

I looked down and saw
her perfect, tiny, five fingered left hand
resting on my foot.
It was a perfect moment.
Two different species, but both your creations,
touching and being touched
without fear.
I can still see her, I can still feel her.
I think I always will.

Discovering my right big toenail was distasteful
she crawled across to my left foot,
but that toenail also failed the test.
Lizards don't appear to shrug their shoulders,
but I think she would've if she could.
Calmly, she wandered down into the garden
and under the house.

You made lizards long before you made humans.
I wonder,
did you look at their tiny, perfect, five fingered hands
and think,
"That is good. I'll do it again".

May we humans show more respect,
more love,
more care,
for our older cousins.
Amen.

ENVIRONMENT

Creator God, Holy One,
you who fashioned our beautiful blue-green planet
and called its many life forms into being,
do you grieve when you look now upon your creation?
Does your heart ache as you gaze upon the dirty skies,
the plastic filled oceans, the poisoned soil?
Do you hold the extinct and dying creatures in your embrace?
Do you again repent that you made humankind?

Have mercy on us, Creator God,
for we have eaten the Eden fruit and we know exactly what we are doing.

Forgive our greed.
Forgive our arrogance.
Forgive our ambition.
Forgive our ideological blindness.
Forgive our laziness.
Forgive our unwillingness to forego even the smallest convenience.

Remind us again that we are but part of the web of life
and totally dependent upon it.
May we have this deep knowing
as individuals,
as communities,
as corporations,
as governments.

Grow within us the wisdom,
the courage,
the humility,
to change our ways
and tread gently upon your earth.

May it be so.

Environment *was composed following the publication of a UN paper on climate change and the Australian Government's rededication to coal.*

EVANGELISM

Good evening, God,
I need to talk with you about evangelism.
You see, I'm a total failure at it;
at least, in the sense in which it is most often used.
When the Holy Spirit was handing out this gift,
I must've been at the back of the line.

I've never "led anyone to Christ".
Yes, I have baptised adults,
but it never seemed to me that I had anything to do with their decision
to take that momentous step.
I think it more likely they just wanted to be part of our lovely congregation.

So, I resonate with those who say that it is more important
to live the gospel and to love people
than to aggressively urge them to convert.

But ... and this is what I really want to talk to you about,
I do wonder why Christians think it so necessary to convert others?

I know Matthew 28:19 says to go and make disciples of all nations,
but does this mean that everyone needs to be converted,
or that converts may be from all nations, Gentiles and not just Jews??
Seems to me it can equally take the latter meaning of total inclusivity,
after all, that is what happened.

And all those theologically mind-blowing "I am" statements in John's gospel!
Surely they are meant to reassure a small, persecuted minority
that they are on the right track,
rather than provide a template for future world domination?

Because, God, and this is probably the heart of the matter,
I simply cannot believe that you condemn people to eternal damnation
because they don't confess Jesus as Lord,
or if they do confess him as Lord, don't say the right things about him.
That path has led to far too much bloodshed and heartache.
Still does, for that matter.

I can hear you asking, "So, what might evangelism be for you?"

Well ...

Perhaps an offer to explore a world view
that connects us with our deepest selves,
with others,
and with Ultimate Reality (that's you).

Perhaps the offer of a lifestyle that works in both joy and sorrow.

Perhaps, with luck, inclusion in a caring community.

Perhaps ...
Please let me know.

FEAR

O God, I'm so frightened.
Fear clutches my heart and tightens my chest.
My breasts tingle.
My daughter, my baby, thinks she has found a lump in her breast.
My mind screams, "No, No, NO!!!"

I've been there,
made that journey,
but, please God, not her,
not my darling girl.

And so I pray
those prayers I used for myself,
over and over until they became the reality I lived from,
live from still.

Later ...
The news is good.
Relief floods in.
The shattered pieces of my world
slide slowly back into place,
and yet ...
why am I still in floods of tears?

The fear is still there.
I have learned yet again
how fragile is our happiness,
how fragile our lives.

Hold us, O God,
Hold us together when everything else is falling apart.

FOR THE EXILES

Holy One, have mercy on your exiles,
those of us who no longer fit
within the traditional teachings of the church.
Those whose voice falters in the songs,
who cannot say "Amen",
who desperately think of something else during the sermon.
Those who think the greatest heresy of all
is to say that you require suffering and death
in order to forgive.
Those who have given up on going to church at all.

Have mercy on us, Holy God,
those exiles who cling to faith
and yearn for a bigger, wider story,
a bigger, wider community.
A story that embraces the vast expanses of time and space,
and the enormous complexity of the cosmos.
A community in which everything and everyone is connected
and embraced.

Holy God, as we approach the Feast of Incarnation,
be born again in us, your exiles;
tell your story in words that we can understand,
create from us a new community.

I hope it may be so.

GOOD FRIDAY

Hello, God.
I went to church today – I was singing in the music team.
The songs and prayers were great,
but ...
yes, I had difficulty with the sermon.

It was one of those,
"Jesus loves us so much he died for us".
"Because Jesus died for us, we know our sins are forgiven."

Why does no-one talk about "WHY?"
Why is forgiveness conditional on this horrific death?

I must say, God,
these sermons don't paint you in a very favourable light.
They make you into a sadistic monster
who must be satisfied with a certain amount of pain
before granting your favour.

You know I don't believe you are like that.

So, I came away from church
thinking about how I see Good Friday.
How do I understand Jesus' death?

The first thing that came to mind was the political aspect;
an act of oppression by the various powers-that-be
to get rid of a perceived dissident.
How about a sermon drawing parallels with today's world?

I also think it is an epiphany,
a showing-forth of your presence with us
even in the worst that life can throw at us.
I like this one.

Later on, when I was walking through the rain forest,
the thought came to me,
"What did Jesus think he was doing?"
Perhaps that is the most important question of all.

The gospels tell us that Jesus chose to go to Jerusalem
even though he knew it would be dangerous.
He knew going there was important
and carefully orchestrated his entry into the city.
He drew comfort from a meal with his closest companions.
What did he think would happen next?

In Gethsemane, he is in great emotional turmoil.
I'm thinking that the temptation to leave was strong.
How easy would it be to call the group together
and say, "I think we better slip away now".
They'd probably heave a sigh of relief.

If I'd been there, I'd be packed already.

But he didn't.
He stayed.
Not because he wanted to,
but because he believed this was what you wanted him to do.
It was an act of radical obedience.

As I was walking along, this stopped me in my tracks.
Radical obedience.

If Jesus would stay to face danger, even death
in witness to the call that you had given him,
to bring good news to the poor,
liberty to the captives,
recovery of sight to the blind,
to let the oppressed go free,
what does that mean for me?

Am I, too, called to this radical obedience,
called to what do what is asked,
even if it is difficult,
even if there is no "happy ending?"

Well, God,
if it was good enough for Jesus,
I suppose it's good enough for me.

IN THE CHAPEL

I said, "O God, where are you?"
The response was so immediate I pulled my shoes from my feet
and bowed down to the ground.

Presence.
Presence.
Presence.
Be assured.
I have called you by name, you are mine.

This is all I need.
This is everything I need.

Our institutions, our organisations, our churches.
Our doctrines.
How small.
How incomplete.

Don't sweat the small stuff.

Amen.

Historic Wesleyan Chapel, Horton Street, Port Macquarie

LENT 5

Isaiah's God, you promise waters in the wilderness,
rivers in the desert,
a way to bring your people home.
It all sounds so neat,
so convenient.
But it's not, is it?

I've seen the TV news,
seen the swirling floods carry away
the detritus of an ordered life.

Rubbish, Paul called it, and he would know.
He jumped into your swirling floods
and let them take away everything
he had ever known or relied on.
What courage!

Is this letting go the way home?
Can I,
will I,
jump
into you?

LETTING GO

God of all, it's hard to let go.
Hard to let go of how I expect life to be,
how life used to be.

Hard to let go of my children,
hard to let them leave the nest and make their own lives.
I rejoice for them, but it is hard.

Hard to let go of my husband, who he used to be.
Hard to remember how he used to be,
how we used to be together.

I'm telling you this not to complain,
but because I know you will understand.

You are a God who has let go,
let go of your beautiful creation,
let go of your hopes and dreams for the world,
let go of us, your wayward children.
I'm sure that is very hard.

So, show me who I am to be
as I let go.

LONDON TOWER BLOCK TRAGEDY (or Ukraine, or Palestine/Israel, or ....)

OK, God, where were you?
Where were you when that building went up like a torch?
Where were you as the families huddled behind hot doors,
clutching their children as the smoke seeped in,
and the walls got hotter,
until finally the flames broke through?
Where were you then?

My brain parrots,
"Jesus said that God is with the sparrow that falls"
while my heart replies, "Yeah, yeah"
and tears well up every time I see the scenes on TV news.

I wish I could get angry.
I know people who seem to live in a state of righteous anger;
but how are they so sure that they are right?
When I get angry, I only make other people angry, or defensive,
or worse still, I hurt those I love.

So, I get sad.
But does that do any good?
Last week, a woman said to me,
"When I think of what they're doing to the Pilliga,
I find it hard to get out of bed".
But she does get out of bed;
I met her at an anti-Adani rally outside the Commbank.
Is she a bit like Jesus,
who wept over Jerusalem, but went there anyway?

Be with us, God.
Be with those desperate families in burning buildings,
war-torn cities and rickety boats.
Be with our aching earth and all its creatures.
Be with that woman as she struggles out of bed.
Be with me as I watch the news with tears running down my cheeks.

LONELY

Hello, God.
I'm lonely, and I need to talk to someone.
It might seem silly to say that I'm lonely
when my lovely husband is here in the house with me,
but I am.

You know why.
We have the same conversations over and over again,
day after day,
and when he asks, "How're you doing?"
it doesn't matter whether I say, "I'm tired, I'm hungry, I'm whatever …"
the response is the same.

I know it isn't his fault, but still,
let's just say it isn't easy.

I've been checking my phone all day
looking for a message from my daughter,
"Hi, Mum, we're going for a walk,
want to come?"
Logically, I know this is not going to happen;
they have weekend guests,
but still I check.

When I went for my walk this afternoon
I chose the busy riverside pathway
hoping I might see someone I know to chat with.
I didn't.

When I got home, George was still napping,
so I made myself a cup of tea and came into my study
to talk with you.

Thank you that I can always talk with you.

LORD OF THE SPHERES

Creator God, when you called matter out of energy,
when atoms formed and split and gases coalesced into spheres
did you delight in what you had made?
Do you laugh as you watch these cosmic spheres whirl through space,
in and around and among each other in a cosmic dance?

We, your human children, like spheres,
beautiful round objects with so many exciting possibilities.

We make spheres of all sizes and textures,
hard, soft, large, small, smooth or fuzzy.
We throw them,
bounce them,
kick them,
juggle them,
and hit them with all sorts of sticks.
We've even squashed them into ovals so we never know
how they will bounce.
We have invented games with complicated rules;
some games even last five days!

Do you delight to see your children at play?
I hope so.

But do you grieve when we turn our games
into fierce, unfriendly competitions?
When we seek to intimidate, hurt and humiliate,
when we treat the other team as "opponents" instead of "partners"
without whom we couldn't play the game.
I expect you do grieve when we do this.

Help us, God of the Spheres,
to play aright.

LUNCH

"God bless the food and drink that I am about to receive,
and please make me truly thankful."

Thank you, also,
for the many people who have brought this food to my table;
the farmers, milkers, processors, pickers, packagers, drivers
and supermarket checkers.
So many people behind my cheese salad sandwich!

Thank you for this abundance.
Thank you that I have always had enough to eat,
enough to feed my children.
Thank you that I never had to worry whether they would live or die.
Thank you.

Thank you that this abundance arises out of peace.
Thank you that war has always been beyond my borders,
that I have always known the blessings of peace.
Thank you that I can drive to the supermarket
and know that it will still be there,
that my home will be waiting for me upon my return.

And thank you for the beauty that surrounds me;
tall trees, flowering plants, buzzing bees, cheeky birds,
over the back fence a kangaroo with her joey begging a slice of bread.
This also is the gift of peace.

So many, many people do not enjoy these gifts of peace.
May I be mindful of them.
May I be helpful to them.

May I be mindful also of our planet
from which this abundance and this beauty flows.
May I do all I can to heal its wounds
and preserve its threatened beauty.

Amen.

MAY I KNOW YOU

Lord Jesus, may I know you.

May I know you on the highways and byways of life.
May I know you as I go about my daily business.
May I know you in car and bus and train.
May I know you in the fleeting glimpses of life flashing by.

May I know you in my family and friends.
May I know you in my colleagues and acquaintances.
May I know you in the people who pass me by on the street.

May I know you in the poor and oppressed.
May I know you in the proud and arrogant.
May I know you in the sinner.
May I know you in the self-righteous.
May I know you in those who weep.
May I know you I those who laugh.

May I know you in the intellect.
May I know you in contemplation.
May I know you in the crowd.
May I know you in solitude.
May I know you in song.
May I know you in dance.
May I know you in the intricacies of the mind's tasks.

Eating and sleeping,
laughing and crying,
alone or with others,
living and dying.
Lord Jesus, may I know you.

This was not written during my seventies but decades before when I was studying at Uniting Theological College. I gave a copy to my dear friend and spiritual partner, Rev. Shirley Parkin, and include it now in its original form in memory of her.

MENTAL HEALTH WEEK

"This is the day that the Lord has made,
we will rejoice and be glad in it."
So goes the psalm, so goes the song.
It's a nice thought,
but not all of us can do it.

Some of us have bodies filled with pain.
Some of us have relationships tumbling down around our ears,
or no relationships at all.
Some of us are wrapped in a cloud of depression so thick
that even the sun feels heavy.

Some of us find it hard just to get out of bed.
Getting through the day is all we can manage,
there's no energy left for rejoicing.

Remember us, O God,
remember those of us who can't rejoice.

Send us someone who will listen, and understand.
Someone who won't tell us to pull ourselves together,
exercise more,
change our diet,
or have more faith.

God, be with us in the heaviness.
Hold us, so that the darkness does not overwhelm.

May it be so.

MOTHER'S DAY

Mother God, I know that I am blessed.
My children are safe and strong,
grown now, with children of their own.

But oh, I miss my little girls, my babies.
I miss their weight in my womb,
their mouth on my breast,
the soft baby smell from the crown of their heads.
I miss their bright faces, their laughter,
their arms around my neck, their voices calling, "Mummy!"
I miss kissing them goodnight and knowing that all is well in my world
because my little girls are here, and safe.

Yet, if I can feel this ache inside,
how then for women who are not so blessed?
Those whose arms have never held a longed-for child.
Those whose child is hungry, hurt or harmed.
Whose child is missing.
Whose child has died.
How great their ache, their pain?

Mother God, mother those women.
Hold them, rock them, sing to them,
let them cry out their pain upon your shoulder.

MUSIC

Wonderful God,
creator of sound and song and the music of the spheres.
Thank you for the gift of music.
Thank you for the gift of my voice.

At the concert the other day, I sang Carmen's "Habanera" – again!
I realised it has been fifty years since I first sang it!
Thank you that, all my life, music has been a joy and treasure.
Thank you that I can still sing.

When I think about dying, one of the things that disturbs me
is that the voice will be stilled;
that separate "something" which is me and yet more than me
will be no more.
I hope not.
I hope that somehow the vibrations will go on and on and on.

I don't want to "die laughing", God.
I want to die singing.

NAIDOC WEEK

God of all the tribes and nations of the earth,
I give you thanks for Australia's First Peoples.
I have so much to learn from them.

All my life, I have been a wanderer upon the face of the earth.
I struggle to understand a sense of bone deep connection with the land,
of having been with the land for tens of thousands of years,
of being one with the land.

I struggle with it.
I yearn for it.

Yet even as I yearn, I glimpse the pain that comes from separation.
I do not know what is like to be torn from my country,
my roots,
my culture,
my language,
my family,
my self.

How many of us turn our eyes away because the pain is too great?
God, forgive us, and give us the strength to turn around, and see.

Strength.
With deepest respect, I give thanks for the strength of Australia's First Peoples.
They have survived.
Against all the odds, against all the good and bad intentions,
they have survived.

But not all.
And not all who are alive today are whole,
many have lost too much.
God, forgive us for what we have done,
for what we continue to do.

I pray for the continued resurgence
of First Peoples' culture, language and pride.
Named or unnamed
you are their strength,
you are their inspiration,
you are in their Law
you sing in their Dreaming.

And out of my own small circle of experience,
I give thanks for the United Aboriginal and Islander Christian Congress;
their insightful theology,
their inspiring worship,
their bright and beautiful young leaders.
May they continue to enrich and heal their peoples.
May they continue to be a gift and inspiration to the whole church.

God of all the tribes and nations of the earth,
I give you thanks for Australia's First Peoples.

Amen.

NEW YEAR

Hello, God.
Today is New Year's Eve,
at least for some of your children;
others honour a different calendar.
But tonight many of us will celebrate
this arbitrary division of time.
Tomorrow we will put up a new calendar,
open up a new diary,
write a new number at the end of the dateline,
and act as if this day is somehow different from the day just past.
Many will make New Year Resolutions,
hopeful statements of intent to be a better person.
Some of us may even keep them,
at least for a while.

Do you look with compassion upon our feverish activity,
knowing that we earthy creatures need our symbols,
need our hopes for new beginnings and better times?

For you are the God of Eternal Now,
in you, past, present and future just ... are.
In you, we don't have to wait for a New Year for a new beginning.
Grace is present, any time, any day, any and every moment,
ever and always ... now.

So here is my New Year Prayer;
May I let go my entanglement with the past,
doing so with love, with forgiveness, with thanksgiving.
May I let go my concern for the future.
May I learn to live in the Eternal Now,
with you.

Yes, let it be so.

NEW ZEALAND, FOLLOWING THE CHRISTCHURCH MOSQUE MASSACRE

Oh God,
my eyes weep and my heart aches
for my brothers and sisters in New Zealand.
How much more must yours?

For people who thought they had come to a place of safety
that illusion is torn away.
A double, a triple grief.
Lord, have mercy.

Have mercy on those who grieve.

Have mercy on those who struggle to recover from wounds
physical, emotional, spiritual.

Have mercy on the community
as they struggle to come to terms and respond
to what has happened.

Have mercy on those who carry out such acts of violence.

Have mercy on us who watch from afar.

Grant us all your peace.

Let it, oh, let it be so.

NO and YES

No.
No has no place in prayer.
No shuts the door, returns the gift.

Yes.
Yes is prayer.
Yes to the Infinite Possibility of God.

Jesus knew that.
His Prayer tumbles Yes upon Yes upon Yes.

Yes removes the shoes with trembling hands
before the burning bush.

No draws the blinds against the night.
Yes walks outside to gaze in awe at the bright infinity above.

No stays on the concrete.
Yes dances bare foot in the grass.

Yes sings the new song.

Yes dares to whisper "I do" in life-long commitment.

No throws down the thirty pieces of silver.

Yes sweats blood in the garden,
Yes rolls away the stone.

Yes is terrifying.

May I say Yes.

OCEAN

Hello, God.
Sometimes I think that you are like the ocean;
vast,
encircling every land mass, large or small.

Source of life;
our very, very ancient ancestors
dared to leave its enfolding.
Why, I wonder, did they leave their Eden?
Even now, the ocean holds life forms beyond human knowledge.

Sustainer of life;
without the oceans, our planet would die.
Might yet die.

God. Ocean.
I have seen a picture of a boat upon the Ocean,
and the boat was depicting the Oikoumene,
the household of God,
the church.

I can relate to that, in a way.

I grew up with the ocean, or at least part of it,
at the end of the garden,
and my friends and I would mess about in boats.
When we go out in a boat,
we experience more of the ocean
than we can on the shore.

When, in my late teens,
I wanted to know more about you, God,
I got into the boat.
I joined the church.

At first, I was a passenger,
and that was great,
I was seeing, hearing, experiencing
so much about you!

Gradually, I became a crew member;
at first a humble puller of an oar,
but diligently I worked my way up
to more complex duties.
Eventually, I became one of those on the bridge;
one who decided how the boat should operate,
which direction it should sail.

And I liked it, you know I did.
I was good at it, too.

So many, many, wonderful experiences,
and I am grateful, and yet ...

It is possible to pay too much attention to the boat
and not enough to the ocean.
It is possible to become too rigid in what we think,
too safe in where we sail.
For me, the boat became too confining.

I'm not in the boat any more, not exactly.
I got onto the life raft and went over the side.

The life raft is still drifting close to the boat,
but lately I'm no longer on the life raft either.
I'm in the water, hanging on to the life raft
by the tips of my fingers.

One day, I'll let go completely, and that's OK,
because it's not the boat that is important,
it is the Ocean.

Taken by Kathy Luck, used with permission

QUANTUM GOD

Hello, God.
Recently, I've been reading about quantum physics.
Well, more like "Quantum for Dummies",
but still
it is so amazing!

Waves that become particles.
Particles that instantly know what's happening to other particles
no matter how far apart they are.
The almost inexplicable power of observation.
The hypothesis of underlying consciousness.

It feels as if science is catching up to an awareness of you,
the great Observer,
the God of Infinite Possibility,
Ultimate Consciousness,
the I AM.

The other day, I was talking with someone
about some aspect of spiritual practice
and I remarked, "And science bears this out".
They replied, "What's science go to do with it?"

It surprised me.
This person,
intelligent,
university educated,
did not share my delight in the coming together
of two great disciplines,
science and theology.

I wonder, how many people are like that?
People who have shut themselves
into just one of these boxes?

People who give no space to the possibility
of further insights, further riches?

I find it sad.

But,
Quantum God,
Eternal Becoming,
Essential Energy of all things,
you hold them too within yourself.

You are so much more than anything we can imagine.
All the names,
doctrines,
allegories,
metaphors,
whatevers,
that we use to describe you;
they are useful in their way,
but they are not necessary.

Ah!

I have just realised that I can let them go ...

I can just relax, and ...
be ...
with you.

REMEMBER!

"I will call to mind the deeds of the Lord.
I will remember your wonders of old;
I will meditate on all your work
and muse on your mighty deeds."*

So prays the psalmist.

But what of those who can't remember – anything?
Those who ask again and again,
"What day is it? What month, what year?"
Who look for the cat who died two years ago.
Who are driven down a familiar street and ask,
"What town are we in?"
"Have we had Christmas yet?"

Remember, O God, those who cannot remember you.

---

* The quote in verse 1 is from Psalm 76:11-12.

UNBELIEF*

Hello, God.
I went to church this morning but I wish I hadn't.
It was one of those times when I felt so disconnected
I wanted to get down and bang my head against the floor.

Does anyone really believe
that you wanted Saul to destroy all the Amalekites,
including women and children?

Do people really believe that you require suffering and death
before granting forgiveness?

Well, I don't.
I can't believe it, for if I did, I couldn't come to church anymore,
couldn't pray.
Sometimes unbelief is good.

Amen ?

---

* Biblical reference is 1 Samuel 15.

WORLD CRISES

"There is neither Jew nor Gentile,
slave nor free,
male nor female,
for all are one in Christ Jesus."

Neither North Korean, nor South Korean,
nor American,
but all are one in Christ Jesus.

How do I respond to my North Korean self,
who hopes that bigger and better weapons
will keep me safe?

How do I respond to my South Korea self,
who fears destruction
through no fault of my own?

How do I respond to my American self,
so like my North Korean self,
who, above all, cannot bear to seem weak or foolish?

How do I pray healing and peace to all these selves
who are one in Christ Jesus?

God of us all, show me,
show us,
the Way.

Amen.

BRING ME A BOTTLE

Bring me a bottle,
that I may pour the glass, swirl the colour, sniff the bouquet
and let the taste linger on my tongue.

Bring me a bottle,
that we may hold erudite conversation
about this "spritely little wine".

Bring me a bottle,
that I may let the liquid linger down my throat
and nestle in my stomach.

Bring me a bottle,
that with merciful swiftness it may slide into my blood stream
and rise to my brain.

Bring me a bottle,
that when you ask me how I am, I may smile and say,
"Doing fine, and you?"

Bring me a bottle,
that we may keep the surface conversation light
and you may turn away without a thought.

Bring me a bottle,
that when the walls of empty rooms close in
I might not notice.

Bring me a bottle,
that when the rising pain tears my heart apart
I no longer beat it down.

Bring me a bottle,
that I might howl my grief and let the tears
run freely down my cheeks.

Bring me a bottle, that I might forget.

Bring me a bottle, that I might sleep.

For God's sake, bring me a bottle.

The first line was given to me in a dream, and next morning when I sat at my computer the poem wrote itself. And no, I hadn't been drinking.

CHEAP GRACE?

Going home was harder than I'd thought.
Not the decision to go back;
after all, if I didn't go back, I would starve,
but what happened when I got there!
The sight of my father running down the road to meet me,
his face suffused with joy.
For me!

Shame.
The painful awareness of unworthiness.
The fine robe a burden to my shoulders.
The ring burning my finger.
The meat a hard, cold lump in my belly.

Fear.
Fear that I'll stuff it up again,
as I'm still me, the one who stuffed it up before.
Those tendencies, those characteristics are still here inside of me.
But my father loves me, in spite of everything!
I never knew before how much he loved me.
If I had, would I have gone?
Probably.
I'm still me.

This deep, deep shame, full self-awareness, what do I do with it?
Can I look me in the face? Every day?
Look that me in the face?
Can I learn to look at me as my father does?

Can I go to my brother and say,
"I will not want, cannot want, what is yours".
Not 'do' not; I'm still me.
If I tell him my shame, will it make a difference?
To him?

My shame can lead to death.
My shame can lead to life.
My father's love makes only one choice possible.

Accepting grace is not always easy.
Perhaps one day it will be, but not today.

The story of the prodigal son is in Luke 15:11-32.

DECISIONS IN HEAVEN
or
HOW DID CHRISTMAS HAPPEN?
A play for Christmas

CAST:
- God the Father — Kind, and quietly authoritative. Wears ordinary clothes, elderly man cardigan.
- God the Son — Eager and idealistic young man. Wears overalls.
- God the Holy Spirit — Busy, well-intentioned woman. Wears flowing skirt and scarf, wafts around.
- Gabriel CEO, Angels Inc. — Restrained and thinks issues through carefully.
- Michael, Commander of the Heavenly Hosts — likes action. wears camouflage.

3 = Trinity, Father, Son and Holy Spirit speaking as One

SCENE: *Stage set for a meeting.*
(Father and HS enter stage right and take their places, followed by Gabriel and Michael.)

Father: Thank you all for coming. *(Pause)* We have called this meeting ... *(Looks around)*
Where's the Son?
We can't discuss a serious matter without the Son.

HS: He was here a moment ago. Shall I go look for him?
You know, that's my job, dashing around the creation, bringing all things together.
(HS starts to waft when Son dashes in breathlessly and takes a seat.)

Son: Sorry I'm late, Dad. But I was working on this marvellous idea for a new galaxy. It's quite different to anything we've done before, and you know how much we like diversity.

Father:	*(patiently)* I'm sure it's a marvellous idea, and yes, we do like diversity.
HS:	But right now we've got our hands full. With humanity – remember?
Son:	*(Contritely)* Oh yes, sorry.
Father:	Now, where were we? *(Clear throat)* Thank you all, again, for coming. We have called this meeting
HS:	So that you can advise us on a very important matter.
Father:	The people down on earth
HS:	Are getting in a terrible mess
Son:	And have all sorts of wrong ideas
Father:	About who we are and what we want them to do.
HS:	So, we have decided
Son:	That I should go down and visit them
Father:	And tell them what we are really like.
HS:	Now what we would like you to help us decide
Father:	Is what size, shape or form
Son:	I should take while I'm down there.
3:	Any suggestions?
Gabriel:	Go down and visit them! In person! Isn't that taking things a bit far?
Michael:	I agree. They're not worth it. Let them stew in their own juice!
Gabriel:	I've said it before but I'll say it again, it was a mistake giving them free will. A real design flaw. *(to Son)* I hope you're not planning on doing that with your new galaxy idea?
Son:	As a matter of fact …
Father:	Gabriel, I'm not having this argument again. Humanity has free will and that's all there is to it. Yes, it makes them unpredictable, but so interesting!
Son:	They're very important to us
HS:	And we want to help them, because
3:	We love them.

Michael: *(reluctantly)* Well, in that case, we'll do our best to help you. Although I still must advise that the risks may outweigh the benefits.

Gabriel: Why don't we just send them a couple of lists You know, one list of things they ought to do, and another list of of things they ought not to do. Surely that would solve the problem?

HS: We're already tried that with Moses. Don't you remember?

Michael: That was a good one. Moses went up the mountain to get the list while all the people waited down below. Don't you remember the thunderstorm I put on for it? *(exuberantly)* Bang!! Boom!! Crash!! That really showed them this list was important.

Gabriel: It can't have been that good or they wouldn't be in such a mess now.

Michael: *(Menace)* It was a terrific thunderstorm!

Gabriel: OK, it was a great thunderstorm, but the list didn't work. Some people don't take any notice of it.

Father: *(sadly)* And even those who do take notice
Son: Have still got it wrong.
HS: We gave them a nice, short, simple list
Son: About being kind to each other
HS: And now they think
Father: I'm more interested in lists than in people.
Son: They've made so many lists
HS: Of things you can do and things you can't do
Father: That there is total confusion!

Michael: Yeah, yeah, I can see the problem.
(to Gabriel) Obviously, another list is not a good idea.

Gabriel: I think a personal visit is a great idea. I love getting visitors.

Son: But what should I go as, that's the question?

Gabriel: Why don't we send him as a priest? The priests are the ones who are supposed to know all about God. Send him as a priest!

Michael: That's the stupidest idea I ever heard of. The reason we have to send him in the first place is because the priests are getting it wrong! We should send him as a king.
That's only right, for someone as important as the Son.

Father: That won't work. Kings down on earth are doing a terrible job.
Son: They're greedy and selfish and don't take care of their people.
HS: We've already warned them of that, and they didn't take any notice.

Gabriel: Then why don't we send him as a very rich man? That way he can use all his money to help others.

Michael: That's not a bad idea ... but what about when the money runs out? Things won't really have changed.
I've got it.
We'll send him as a great soldier who **makes** people do the right thing. Someone like Sylvester Stallone
(Acts out shooting people. Make lots of noise)
3: Order! Order! Order!

Son: There are too many soldiers down there already.
HS: People kill each other all the time.
Father: And it makes things worse, not better!
(short pause)
Son: Why don't I go as just an ordinary person?
All: What?

Son: I said, why don't I go as just an ordinary person?
Father: Hmmm, let me think. That way they will know that we love everyone
HS: Not just the important people.

Michael: You mean, you would live just an ordinary life, among ordinary people?
How would that help?

Gabriel: Well, if he was an ordinary person he could talk to them in ordinary words and they might understand more easily.

Son: Yes, but I wouldn't just **tell** them, I'd **show** them.

Gabriel/Michael: That might just work.

HS; I've thought of something else, something important
All: What?

HS: If he becomes an ordinary person, we will know, from the inside, what it's like to be one of them.
Son: That's exactly right!
Father: *(nods thoughtfully)* That's important. In fact, it's so important, I might have thought of it myself.

(pause)

Son: But, how will I get there?

Michael: Go down in a chariot of fire in a great big thunderstorm. Bang! Crash! Boom!

Gabriel: No! No more thunderstorms!

Father: It seems to me that if he's to be an ordinary person,
HS: he ought to be born like every other ordinary person.
Son I should go as a baby.

ALL: A baby!

(Father, Son and HS listen and nod during the following dialogue)

Gabriel: No-one would expect that.
Michael: How would they know who he was?
Gabriel: It could be risky.
Michael: Not to say downright dangerous!
Gabriel: Babies are so little ...
Michael: So helpless ...
Gabriel: They can't do anything for themselves.
Michael: He'd grow up just like an ordinary kid.
Gabriel: He'd have to learn everything all over again.
Michael: How to walk.
Gabriel: How to talk.
Michael: He'd have to go to school.
Gabriel: And get a job.
Michael: He'd be just like an ordinary person
Gabriel/Michael Fancy the Son being like that.

(pause)

HS: It would be wonderful.
(pause)

Michael: But it would be very, very dangerous. Human beings are very unpredictable, even violent.

Gabriel: I think, taking all things into consideration, I must advise against it.

Father: Son, you've heard all they've said. It'll be dangerous. Will you risk it? Will you go as just an ordinary baby?

Son: Yes, Dad. I'll go.

HS: Oh, are you sure? I know it's a wonderful idea, but if something bad should happen to you

Father: *(with great emotion)* It will break our heart.
(pause)

Son: Perhaps **that** is what they need to know.

(Father and HS wrap their arms around the Son, and they exit, followed by Gabriel and Michael.)

This was originally written in 1994 for my Years 5/6 Special Religious Education class. That version had enough angels to give every child a speaking part! When asked in 2020 to provide a Christmas play for the local church, I revised the play and it was performed during Advent 4 worship.

WHAT IS PRAYER?

I suppose the answer to that question depends
on our understanding of God.
Or perhaps I can put it the other way;
often we can surmise someone's understanding of God
by how they pray.

Some prayers are like a Letter to Santa Claus,
a list of things wanted.
If the requested "present" arrives,
then it is assumed that God is pleased with the request
and, by inference, the pray-er has been a good person
with the correct amount of faith.

This may seem quite a child-like way to pray,
but the more adult version, the Shopping List,
works in much the same manner.
In this version, God is like the Shop Keeper
who may or may not supply the desired item.

If the requested "present" does not arrive
or is not in the Shop,
there are a number of coping strategies.

A favourite seems to be that "Now is not yet the right time",
like the present being delayed in the post.

Another is that God knows best,
the request was incorrect and therefore will not be granted.

If we're praying for a rise in salary or a new car,
these rationalisations may work quite well,
but if the prayer is for something serious,
perhaps healing or freedom from pain,
they are a bit thin.

That's where the dreaded insinuation that either the pray-er,
or the pray-ee,
don't have enough faith might creep in,
adding guilt to the existing problem.

Another type of prayer is the Board Report,
which majors in telling God, the CEO, about the situation.
These prayers go into great detail about the present problem,
(as if God doesn't already know)
but very little is said about the desired result.

For example:

"We pray for Mary, who is having a difficult time right now.
Her hip is so painful it is really hard for her to get around.
The specialist said she needs a hip replacement,
but what with Covid and all
the waiting list has blown right out
and it looks as if it might be another 12 to 18 months
before she can have the surgery.
So, Lord, we pray for Mary."

What we are actually praying for Mary is left unspecified,
which in one sense is a good tactic
since whatever happens, even if it is nothing,
the prayer can be said to be answered,
although if Mary is actually present when this is prayed
she might feel even more weighed down than before.

Sometimes, the Board Report does recommend to the CEO
what actions are required to address the situation
and, again, usually no detail is spared.

The coping strategies used for the unanswered Letter to Santa Claus
work equally well for the disregarded Board Report.

A less depressing version of the Board Report
is the News Update
which simply mentions the names of those being prayed for
without going into any details.

So, what is prayer for me?
I don't think I pray **to** so much as pray **with**.
That's what this collection of writings is all about.
I have named God as
Ocean,
Quantum God,

Eternal Becoming,
Essential Energy,
Great Observer
Infinite Possibility,
Ultimate Consciousness,
The I AM.
Or, more biblically,
the One in whom we live and move and have our being.

The task of prayer, therefore, is to become aware of that Presence,
that Energy,
that Infinite Possibility,
within and around and through me.
It is to be open,
to say "Yes",
to be still and know.

The Apostle Paul said, "Pray at all times"
and I don't think he meant words.
I think he meant that openness,
that "Yes",
that participation in an Energy that can, and does,
change everything.

Some people think that if you are not asking a definite Person to do something,
it's not prayer.
Other people seem to think that since God is already present and knowing,
there's no need to pray.
But I think that if prayer is deliberate participation in the Energy of God,
humbly offering a pathway
through which that Energy may flow in a more concentrated fashion,
prayer is more important than ever.

When I pray for another person or situation,
I try to hold them with me in that space,
in that energy,
so that Possibility may become reality.
And yes, some things are too immense for my small space of holding,
but joined with other small spaces, who knows,
we may open a window wide enough
for a new Becoming.

www.ingramcontent.com/pod-product-compliance
Lightning Source LLC
Chambersburg PA
CBHW012009090526
44590CB00026B/3936